Travel Guide

NEW ZEALAND

2023 EDITION

TABLE OF CONTENTS

INTRODUCTION
WELCOME TO NEW ZEALAND

Welcome to New Zealand, a land of breathtaking scenery, rare wildlife, and a rich cultural heritage. New Zealand, located in the southwestern Pacific Ocean, is a country of natural beauty and adventure, providing visitors with a once-in-a-lifetime experience.

The diverse landscapes of New Zealand are breathtaking, from the breathtaking mountain ranges of the Southern Alps to the stunning fjords of Milford Sound. Hiking through lush rainforests, skiing on snow-capped peaks, and relaxing on pristine beaches are all options for visitors.New Zealand also has a diverse range of flora and fauna, such as the iconic kiwi bird and the ancient kauri tree.

And, with a rich history spanning both Maori and European cultures, the country provides an intriguing glimpse into its past and present.

New Zealand has something for everyone, whether you're looking for adventure, relaxation, or cultural immersion. We'll take you on a journey through the country's must-see destinations, provide insider tips on the best places to eat, drink, and stay, and help you plan the trip of a lifetime in this travel guide. So pack your bags and get ready to discover New Zealand's wonders!

BRIEF HISTORY OF NEW ZEALAND

New Zealand has a long and complex history that dates back thousands of years. The Maori were the first inhabitants of the Islands, arriving from Polynesia around 1000 AD. The Maori developed a sophisticated culture that placed a strong emphasis on tribal identity and spiritual beliefs. Abel Tasman, a Dutch explorer, was the first European to discover New Zealand in 1642, but he was met with hostility from the Maori and did not attempt to establish a permanent settlement. It wasn't until 1769 that the British navigator James Cook arrived in New Zealand and began mapping the Islands.

European settlers began to arrive in greater numbers in the early nineteenth century, drawn by the promise of land and resources. This resulted in conflicts with the Maori, who were increasingly marginalized and deprived of their traditional lands. The Treaty of Waitangi was signed in 1840 by the British Crown and Maori chiefs, but it was not always faithfully implemented, resulting in ongoing tension and conflict between Maori and Pakeha (non-Maori) communities.

In the late nineteenth and early twentieth centuries, New Zealand became increasingly integrated into the global economy, with agriculture and dairy farming becoming economic mainstays. The country also played an important role in both World Wars, with many New Zealanders serving in the armed forces abroad.

With the establishment of a welfare state and the growth of a more diverse and multicultural society in the postwar period, New Zealand underwent significant social and economic changes.

The establishment of national parks and protected areas elevated the country to the forefront of environmental conservation and sustainability.

Today, New Zealand is a thriving democracy with a diverse and dynamic economy, a rich cultural heritage, and a reputation as one of the most beautiful and welcoming countries in the world.

LOCATION AND SIZE OF NEW ZEALAND

Geography and Location:

New Zealand is a country located in the southwestern Pacific Ocean. It consists of two main Islands, the North Island and the South Island, as well as numerous smaller Islands. The North Island and South Island are separated by the Cook Strait, which is approximately 22 kilometers (14 miles) wide at its narrowest point.

The total land area of New Zealand is approximately 268,021 square kilometers (103,483 square miles), making it slightly larger than the United Kingdom and slightly smaller than Japan.

The North Island is the smaller of the two Islands, with a land area of approximately 113,729 square kilometers (43,911 square miles), while the South Island is larger, with a land area of approximately 151,215 square kilometers (58,384 square miles).

New Zealand is located about 2,000 kilometers (1,243 miles) east of Australia across the Tasman Sea. Its closest neighbors are Australia to the west, Fiji and Tonga to the north, and New Caledonia to the northeast. Due to its location in the southern hemisphere, the seasons in New Zealand are opposite those in the northern hemisphere, with summer lasting from December to February and winter from June to August.

8

Size and Population:

New Zealand has a total land area of approximately 268,021 square kilometers (103,483 square miles), making it slightly larger than the United Kingdom and slightly smaller than Japan. The North Island is the smaller of the two Islands, with a land area of approximately 113,729 square kilometers (43,911 square miles), while the South Island is larger, with a land area of approximately 151,215 square kilometers (58,384 square miles).

As of 2021, the estimated population of New Zealand is approximately 5 million people. The majority of the population lives in urban areas, with approximately 1.7 million people living in Auckland, the country's largest city. Other major cities in New Zealand include Wellington, the capital city, Christchurch, and Dunedin.

The population of New Zealand is diverse, with a mix of Maori, European, Pacific Islander, and Asian ethnicities. Approximately 15% of the population identifies as Maori, while the largest European ethnic group is of British

descent. The Pacific Islander community, which includes people from Samoa, Tonga, and Fiji, makes up approximately 8% of the population, while the Asian community, which includes people from China, India, and the Philippines, makes up approximately 16% of the population.

New Zealand is a relatively sparsely populated country, with a population density of approximately 18 people per square kilometer. The majority of the population is concentrated in the North Island and the major urban centers, while much of the South Island is rural and sparsely populated.

OVERVIEW OF NEW ZEALAND CULTURE

New Zealand's culture is distinct and diverse, shaped by the country's history, geography, and people. New Zealand's culture is a mash-up of Maori, European, Pacific Islander, and Asian influences, resulting in a rich tapestry of traditions, values, and customs.

The traditional Maori culture, which is still very much alive today, is one of the most important aspects of New Zealand culture. The Maori people were New Zealand's first inhabitants, and their culture had a significant impact on the country's history and identity.

Maori traditions and customs are woven into the fabric of everyday life in New Zealand, and visitors are frequently greeted with a powhiri, a traditional Maori welcome.

The outdoor lifestyle is another important aspect of New Zealand culture. New Zealand's stunning natural scenery and mild climate provide ample opportunities for outdoor recreation, such as hiking, camping, skiing, and water sports. Kiwis, as New Zealanders are known, are passionate about outdoor activities and spending time in nature, which is reflected in the country's laid-back and welcoming culture.

Sports are also popular in New Zealand, particularly rugby union and cricket. Rugby is considered New Zealand's national sport, and the country's national rugby team, the All Blacks, is one of the most successful and well-known sports teams in the world. New Zealanders are also big cricket fans, and the game is played and watched all over the country.

New Zealand cuisine is influenced by a number of cultures, including European, Maori, and Asian. Fish and chips, meat pies, and pavlova, a meringue and fruit dessert, are among the most popular dishes in New Zealand. New Zealand is also well-known for its wine, particularly Sauvignon Blanc, which is grown in the South Island's Marlborough region.

With a thriving music, film, and visual arts scene, the arts are also an important part of New Zealand culture. Lorde, Crowded House, and Split Enz are among the successful musicians from New Zealand, as are acclaimed

filmmakers Peter Jackson and Taika Waititi.

Finally, the people of New Zealand are known for being friendly and welcoming. Kiwis are generally laid-back and informal, and visitors frequently comment on the country's warmth and hospitality. This welcoming attitude is mirrored in the country's tourism industry, which accounts for a significant portion of the New Zealand economy.

To summarize, New Zealand culture is a rich and diverse mix of traditions, values, and customs derived from a variety of different influences. New Zealand has a unique and vibrant culture that is both fascinating and welcoming to visitors, from its Maori heritage and love of the outdoors to its passion for sports, food, and the arts.

PRACTICAL INFORMATION

BEST TIME TO VISIT NEW ZEALAND

SUMMER (DECEMBER - FEBRUARY)

- This is peak tourist season in New Zealand with warm and sunny weather.
- Ideal for outdoor activities such as hiking, camping, kayaking, and water sports.
- The beaches are ideal for swimming and sunbathing.
- It's a great time to explore the national parks and other scenic attractions.
- This is the busiest and most expensive time to visit New Zealand.

AUTUMN/FALL (MARCH - MAY)

- Weather is mild and pleasant, with fewer tourists and lower prices.
- This is the harvest season, with lots of food and wine festivals taking place.
- The changing colors of the leaves make it a beautiful time for hiking and outdoor activities.
- It's a great time for photography, with the landscape transformed by autumnal hues.

WINTER (JUNE - AUGUST)

- The winter season is ideal for skiing, snowboarding, and other winter sports.
- The ski resorts are in full swing, and there are plenty of opportunities for snow activities.
- This is a great time to enjoy hot springs and thermal baths.
- It's also the best time to see the stunning Southern Lights.

SPRING (SEPTEMBER - NOVEMBER)

- Weather is mild and pleasant, with fewer tourists and lower prices.
- This is a great time for outdoor activities such as hiking, cycling, and wildlife watching.
- The flowers and wildlife are in full bloom, making it an ideal time for photography.
- This is also a great time to experience New Zealand's rich cultural heritage with many festivals and events taking place.

HOW TO GET TO NEW ZEALAND

New Zealand is a remote Island nation located in the South Pacific, but it's still relatively easy to get there from many parts of the world. Here are some ways to get to New Zealand:

By Air:

The most common mode of transportation to New Zealand is by air. Many international destinations, including Australia, Asia, North America, and Europe, have direct flights to New Zealand. Auckland, Wellington, and Christchurch are New Zealand's main international airports, with several smaller airports also serving international flights.

By Land:

While driving to New Zealand from Australia is technically possible, it requires a lengthy journey by ferry or private yacht and is not a practical option for most visitors.

By Sea:

New Zealand is a popular stop for cruise ships, and several major cruise lines offer itineraries that include New Zealand stops. Auckland, Wellington, and Christchurch are the main cruise ports in New Zealand.

VISA REQUIREMENTS

Whether you need a visa to enter New Zealand depends on your nationality and the purpose and length of your stay. Here's an overview of the visa requirements for visiting New Zealand:

Visa Waiver Countries:

Citizens of some countries can visit New Zealand for up to 90 days without a visa, as long as they have a valid passport and a return ticket. These countries include the United States, the United Kingdom, Canada, Australia, and many European countries. Check the New Zealand Immigration website to see if your country is on the list.

Visitor Visa

If you are not from a visa-free country or intend to stay in New Zealand for more than 90 days, you must apply for a visitor visa. This visa allows you to stay in New Zealand for up to 9 months for tourism, visiting friends and family, or participating in other recreational activities. You must show proof of your travel plans, accommodation, and financial means to support yourself during your stay.

It's important to check the visa requirements and application process well in advance of your trip, as it can take several weeks or even months to process your application. Make sure to have all the necessary documents and meet the requirements before you apply for a visa to ensure a smooth and stress-free travel experience.

CURRENCY AND PAYMENT METHODS

1. **Currency Exchange:** Currency exchange for New Zealand dollars can be done at banks, currency exchange offices, and some hotels. It is advisable to compare exchange rates before converting money as they are subject to fluctuations.

2. **Credit and Debit Cards:** In New Zealand, credit and debit cards are commonly used and accepted, particularly in urban regions. Writer, Visa and Mastercard are widely accepted, while American Express and Diners Club are accepted in select locations. Credit card transactions may incur a surcharge at certain businesses.

3. **Cash:** In New Zealand, cash is still widely accepted, particularly in smaller towns and rural regions. New Zealand dollars can be withdrawn from ATMs by using a debit or credit card. It is advisable to confirm with your bank if they charge a fee for international transactions, although the majority of ATMs do accept international cards.

4. **Travelers' Cheques:** Travelers' cheques are not widely used in New Zealand, and some businesses may not accept them. It's better to carry cash or use a credit or debit card instead.

5. **Mobile Payment:** Mobile payment apps like Apple Pay and Google Pay are becoming more popular in New Zealand, and some businesses accept these forms of payment.

It's a good idea to carry a mix of cash and cards when traveling in New Zealand, especially if you plan to visit rural areas where credit card acceptance may be limited. Make sure to notify your bank before you travel to New Zealand to avoid any issues with your cards.

LANGUAGE AND COMMUNICATION

New Zealand's official languages are English, Mori, and New Zealand Sign Language. If you speak English, you should have no trouble communicating with locals, as English is the most widely spoken language. Here is some information about New Zealand's language and communication:

- **English Language:** In New Zealand, English is widely spoken and understood. You will be able to communicate with the majority of the population in English, and all official documents and signs are written in English.

- **Māori Language:** Māori is an official language of New Zealand, so you may encounter Māori words and phrases in everyday speech. Nonetheless, the majority of New Zealanders do not speak Māori fluently.

- **New Zealand Sign Language:** New Zealand Sign Language is also an official language of New Zealand, and it is used by the community of the people with hearing loss.

- **Communication:** You should have no difficulty communicating with locals, as New Zealanders are generally warm and hospitable. Don't be afraid to ask for clarification if you have trouble understanding accents or local slang.

- **Internet and Phone:** In New Zealand, the majority of hotels, cafes, and restaurants offer free Wi-Fi, and you can purchase a prepaid SIM card for your phone if you need to stay connected while traveling. +64 is New Zealand's country code.

English is widely spoken and understood in New Zealand, so communication should not be a problem when traveling there. If you want to connect with the local culture, learning some basic Māori words and phrases can be a fun way to do so.

LOCAL TRANSPORTATION OPTIONS

01 Buses:

You can purchase bus tickets online, at the bus station, or on the bus (cash only) with a credit card or cash. Some bus companies offer discounts for purchasing tickets in advance, and others offer bus passes, which can be a cost-effective way to travel if multiple trips are planned.

- InterCity offers a FlexiPass, which allows you to prepay for a certain number of hours of travel that can be used at any time.
- Naked Bus offers a MegaBus Pass, which allows you to travel between two specified locations as many times as you want within a set period of time.
- ManaBus offers a SuperFlex Pass, which allows you to travel between any two locations on their network at any time within a set period of time.

02 Car Rentals

Prices for car rentals vary based on the type of vehicle and rental company. Most car rental companies require a credit card for payment and a valid driver's license. You can reserve a rental vehicle online or at the airport upon arrival.

03 Trains

Tickets for trains can be purchased online, at train stations, or on board. Some train companies offer discounts for advanced booking, as well as rail passes that permit unlimited travel within a specified time period.

04 Ferries

Ferry tickets are available online, at ferry terminals, and on board. Some ferry companies offer discounts for advanced reservations, and others offer multi-trip passes that can save you money if you intend to make multiple trips.

ACCOMODATIONS

New Zealand offers a variety of accommodation options to accommodate all budgets and travel preferences. Here is a summary of the most common types of accommodation in the country:

Hotels and Resorts:

There are a variety of hotels and resorts in New Zealand, ranging from five-star luxury to more affordable three-star options. Numerous hotels and resorts offer breathtaking views of the surrounding mountains, lakes, or beaches. These accommodations typically include spas, restaurants, and fitness centers.

Bed and Breakfasts:

Bed and breakfasts (B&Bs) are a popular lodging option for those seeking a more personalized experience. B&Bs are typically run by locals and provide a comfortable, homey atmosphere as well as a home-cooked breakfast in the morning.

Holiday Homes:

Holiday homes are a popular option for traveling families and groups. These residences range in size and design, from cozy cottages to expansive villas. They feature a fully equipped kitchen, allowing guests to cook their own meals and enjoy a more independent stay.

Hostels:

Hostels are a budget-friendly option for solo travelers or those looking to save on accommodation costs. Hostels offer shared dormitory-style rooms, as well as private rooms, and often have communal kitchens and lounges.

Camping:

New Zealand has a well-established network of campsites and holiday parks, making it easy for visitors to explore the great outdoors. Camping options range from basic campsites to fully equipped camping grounds with facilities such as showers and kitchens.

The cost of accommodation in New Zealand can vary significantly based on the type of accommodation, location, and season. Prices can range from approximately NZD $10 to NZD $500 per night, depending on the type of accommodation and level of luxury. Always book in advance, especially during peak season, to guarantee availability and get the best rates.

SOME POPULAR HOTELS IN NEW ZEALAND

THE GRAND BY SKYCITY

This luxury hotel is located in the heart of Auckland's CBD and offers a range of stylish rooms and suites with views of the city or harbor. Prices start from around NZD $500 per night.

HILTON AUCKLAND

This waterfront hotel boasts stunning views of Waitemata Harbour and is within walking distance of the city's top attractions. Prices start from around NZD $450 per night.

SOFITEL AUCKLAND VIADUCT HARBOUR

This 5-star hotel is located in the heart of the city's vibrant Viaduct Harbour precinct and offers luxurious rooms and suites with stunning harbor views. Prices start from around NZD $550 per night.

QT WELLINGTON

This quirky and stylish hotel is located in the heart of Wellington and offers a range of unique rooms and suites. Prices start from around NZD $450 per night.

RYDGES WELLINGTON

This modern hotel is located in the heart of the city's CBD and offers stylish rooms and suites with views of the harbor or city. Prices start from around NZD $400 per night.

THE GEORGE HOTEL (CHRISTCHURCH)

This boutique hotel is located in the heart of Christchurch and offers a range of elegant rooms and suites with garden or park views. Prices start from around NZD $300 per night.

NOVOTEL CHRISTCHURCH CATHEDRAL SQUARE

This modern hotel is located in the heart of Christchurch's CBD and offers comfortable rooms and suites with city views. Prices start from around NZD $150 per night.

CROWNE PLAZA QUEENSTOWN

This stylish hotel is located in the heart of Queenstown and offers stunning views of Lake Wakatipu and the Remarkables mountain range. Prices start from around NZD $300 per night

HERITAGE QUEENSTOWN

This luxury hotel is located in a peaceful alpine setting, just a short walk from the heart of Queenstown. It offers spacious rooms and suites with stunning views of Lake Wakatipu and the surrounding mountains. Prices start from around NZD $300 per night.

MILLENNIUM HOTEL QUEENSTOWN

This centrally located hotel offers comfortable rooms and suites with stunning views of Lake Wakatipu and the Remarkables mountain range. Prices start from around NZD $200 per night.

SOME POPULAR
BED AND BREAKFAST (B&B)
IN NEW ZEALAND

EDEN PARK BED AND BREAKFAST (AUCKLAND)

BRAEMAR ON PARLIAMENT STREET (WELLINGTON)

HARBOUR VIEW COTTAGE BED AND BREAKFAST (WELLINGTON)

STONELEIGH LODGE (NAPIER)

THE CLAREMONT (MARTINBOROUGH)

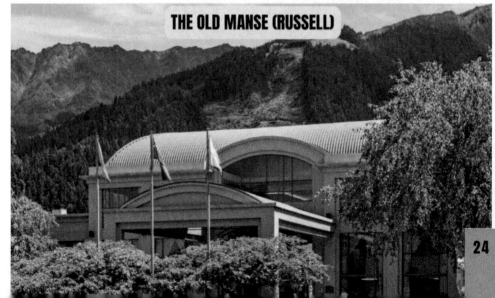

THE OLD MANSE (RUSSELL)

The **White House Bed and Breakfast** is located in a quiet Christchurch suburb and offers elegant rooms with private bathrooms. It is also close to local attractions such as the Christchurch Botanic Gardens and the Canterbury Museum.

Sails Ashore Lodge - On Stewart Island, this charming lodge offers cozy rooms with stunning sea views and is a great base for exploring the island's rugged natural beauty and unique wildlife.

The Waters Bed and Breakfast - Located in Nelson's tranquil garden setting, this B&B offers spacious rooms with private decks and is close to local attractions such as Abel Tasman National Park and Nelson Lakes National Park.

The Guesthouse at Taiharuru Farms Lodge - This opulent B&B in Whangarei offers stylish rooms with panoramic sea views, as well as easy access to nearby beaches and hiking trails.

Hulbert House - This beautifully restored Victorian villa in the heart of Queenstown offers elegant rooms with antique furnishings and is just a short walk from the town's shops, restaurants, and attractions.

Hacorn Estate Motel and Bed and Breakfast - Located near the Botanic Gardens, Canterbury Museum, and Christchurch Cathedral, this Christchurch B&B offers comfortable rooms with garden views.

Villa Walton Bed and Breakfast - Set in a historic villa with lovely gardens, this Tauranga B&B provides comfortable rooms with modern amenities, as well as easy access to local beaches and attractions.

Tuscany on Thames - Inspired by the beauty of Tuscany, this charming B&B in Thames offers stylish rooms with garden views, as well as easy access to local wineries, beaches, and hiking trails.

Almyra Waterfront Lodge - On the shores of Lake Te Anau, this lodge offers spacious rooms with stunning lake views and is an excellent base for exploring the nearby Fiordland National Park and Milford Sound.

SOME POPULAR FAMILY-FRIENDLY HOTELS IN NEW ZEALAND

Novotel Auckland Ellerslie - This Auckland hotel has family rooms with king-size beds, a sofa bed, and a flat-screen TV. There is an indoor heated pool and a restaurant on-site.

Oaks Wellington Hotel - Located in Wellington, this hotel provides spacious family rooms with a kitchenette, a dining area, and a flat-screen TV. There's an indoor pool, a gym, and a restaurant.

Holiday Inn Rotorua - This Rotorua hotel has family rooms with a king-size bed, a sofa bed, and a flat-screen TV. There is a restaurant, an indoor pool, and a hot tub.

Crowne Plaza Queenstown - This Queenstown hotel provides family rooms with a king-size bed, a sofa bed, and a flat-screen TV. There is a restaurant on-site, as well as a free shuttle service to the town center.

The Rees Hotel and Luxury Apartments - Located in Queenstown, this hotel provides spacious family apartments with a kitchen, dining area, and flat-screen TV. There is a restaurant on-site, a private beach, and a shuttle service to the town center.

Sudima Christchurch Airport - This Christchurch hotel provides family rooms with a king-size bed, a sofa bed, and a flat-screen TV. There is a restaurant, an indoor pool, and a fitness center on-site.

Scenic Hotel Te Pania - This Napier hotel has family rooms with a king-size bed, a sofa bed, and a flat-screen TV. There is a restaurant and a pool on-site.

Heritage Queenstown - This Queenstown hotel provides family rooms with a king-size bed, a sofa bed, and a flat-screen TV. There is a restaurant on-site, as well as a free shuttle service to the town center.

CityLife Auckland - This Auckland hotel provides family rooms with a king-size bed, a sofa bed, and a flat-screen TV. There is a restaurant and a fitness center on-site.

Distinction Dunedin Hotel - Located in Dunedin, this hotel provides family rooms with a king-size bed, a sofa bed, and a flat-screen TV. There is a restaurant on-site, as well as a fitness center and a shuttle service to the town center.

PEOPLE & CULTURE
FOOD & DRINKS
AND NIGHTLIFE IN NEW ZEALAND

PEOPLE & CULTURE

The indigenous Mori people, as well as the influence of European and Pacific Island cultures, have shaped New Zealand's rich and diverse culture. The country has a population of about 5 million people, the majority of whom are of European descent, with Mori, Pacific Islander, and Asian communities following.

Traditional practices such as haka (a type of ceremonial dance), waiata (singing), and the use of te reo Mori (the Mori language) are still widely celebrated and embraced in New Zealand. Mori people have a strong connection to the land and the environment, which is reflected in conservation efforts and a focus on sustainable living.

FOOD & DRINKS

The location and natural resources of New Zealand have a strong influence on its food culture. Seafood, lamb, and beef are all popular ingredients in classic dishes like New Zealand meat pie and fish and chips. In recent years, the country's wine industry has grown rapidly, with regions such as Marlborough and Hawke's Bay producing world-class wines.

When it comes to beverages, New Zealand is well-known for its craft beer scene, with a number of local breweries producing one-of-a-kind and delectable beers. The country is also known for its love of coffee, as evidenced by the abundance of cafes and coffee shops found throughout the country.

Bluff oysters

Fish and Chips

A delicacy of New Zealand's South Island, Bluff oysters are plump and juicy with a distinctive briny flavor. They are typically eaten raw or lightly cooked.

This classic dish of battered fish and fries is a favorite across New Zealand. It's often served with tartar sauce and wrapped in paper for a traditional takeaway experience.

Hangi

Hokey pokey ice cream

A traditional Maori cooking method, hangi involves placing food such as meat, vegetables, and potatoes in a pit lined with hot stones and covered with earth. The result is a smoky, tender feast that's often served at cultural events and special occasions.

A creamy vanilla ice cream with small chunks of honeycomb toffee mixed in. It's a popular dessert in New Zealand and is often served with pavlova.

Kiwifruit

A small, brown, fuzzy fruit that is native to New Zealand. It has a bright green flesh that is juicy and sweet, with a slightly tangy flavor.

Kumara (sweet potato)

A staple vegetable in New Zealand cuisine, kumara is a type of sweet potato that has a bright orange flesh and a sweet, nutty flavor. It's often used in soups, stews, and roasted vegetable dishes.

Kina

A local New Zealand seafood delicacy also known as sea urchin. These spiky creatures are harvested from the sea and their roe is considered a delicacy in New Zealand cuisine. Kina is often eaten raw, straight from the shell, or used as a garnish on top of seafood dishes.

L & P

Short for "Lemon & Paeroa," L&P is a sweet, lemon-flavored soda that's been popular in New Zealand since the early 20th century.

Mānuka Honey

Made from the nectar of the mānuka tree, which is native to New Zealand, this honey has gained worldwide recognition for its unique flavor and health benefits.

Marmite

A yeast-based spread that is similar to Vegemite. It's a popular breakfast spread in New Zealand and is often eaten on toast or crackers.

Mussels fritters

Pavlova

The dish consists of fresh mussels mixed with a batter made from flour, eggs, milk, and seasoning, then deep-fried until golden and crispy. The result is a savory and satisfying dish with a crispy outer layer and a tender and juicy mussel center. Mussels fritters are often served with a squeeze of lemon and a side of dipping sauce, such as aioli or tartar sauce.

A dessert that's become an iconic part of New Zealand cuisine, pavlova is a meringue-based dessert that's topped with whipped cream and fresh fruit. It's said to have originated in Australia, but New Zealanders have claimed it as their own.

Pie

Venison

A savory pastry filled with meat, vegetables, and gravy. Popular varieties include steak and cheese, mince and cheese, and bacon and egg.

New Zealand is known for its high-quality venison, which is lean and flavorful thanks to the country's natural grazing pastures. It's often served grilled or in stews and casseroles.

Whitebait Fritters

Crayfish

Green-Lipped Mussels

Greenlip mussels, also known as New Zealand mussels, are a popular New Zealand seafood delicacy. They are large and plump, with a distinctive greenish tinge around the edges of their shells.

Lamb

Anzac Biscuit

Anzac Biscuits are a traditional sweet biscuit made in New Zealand and Australia during World War I. Rolling oats, coconut, flour, sugar, butter, golden syrup, bicarbonate of soda, and boiling water are used to make them. The biscuits are crisp on the outside and chewy on the inside, and they go well with a cup of tea.

Lamington

Lamington is a traditional New Zealand dessert. It consists of a sponge cake cut into squares, layered with chocolate sauce, and rolled in desiccated coconut. To add flavor and moisture, the cake is usually filled with jam or cream.

NIGHTLIFE IN NEW ZEALAND

The nightlife in New Zealand varies depending on location and time of year but there are plenty of options for those looking to have a good time after dark.

There are numerous bars and nightclubs in major cities such as Auckland Wellington, and Christchurch that cater to a wide range of tastes and preferences. The Viaduct Harbour and Ponsonby Road are popular nightlife areas in Auckland, while Cuba Street and Courtenay Place are popular nightlife destinations in Wellington.

Queenstown is also known for its nightlife scene, which includes a variety of bars and clubs, many of which are located on Shotover Street. The city is especially lively during the winter months, when it is a popular skiing and snowboarding destination.

There are plenty of alternatives to traditional bars and nightclubs for those looking for something different. In Auckland, for example, the K'Road area is home to a number of LGBTQ+ friendly bars and clubs, whereas in Wellington there are several live music venues that feature local and international acts.

It should be noted that the legal drinking age in New Zealand is 18, and bars and clubs may ask for identification to verify age. It's also critical to drink responsibly and plan a safe way home after a night out.

TOP TOURIST ATTRACTIONS

Abel Tasman National Park

The South Island's Abel Tasman National Park offers a variety of outdoor activities such as hiking, kayaking, and swimming in the turquoise waters.

Bay of Islands

The Bay of Islands, located on the North Island, is a subtropical paradise. It has beautiful beaches, clear water, and breathtaking scenery. Swimming, kayaking, and snorkeling are among the water activities available to visitors.

Fox Glacier

A glacier on the South Island that visitors can hike on or take a helicopter tour of.

Franz Josef Glacier

The Franz Josef Glacier on the West Coast of the South Island is a popular tourist destination. Visitors can experience the glacier up close by hiking or taking a helicopter tour.

Milford Sound

Milford Sound, located in the Fiordland National Park, is one of New Zealand's most popular tourist destinations. By boat or kayak, visitors can take in the breathtaking scenery of towering cliffs, waterfalls, and sparkling blue water.

Mount Cook National Park

Located in the central South Island, this park is home to New Zealand's highest mountain, Mount Cook, and many hiking trails and alpine vistas.

Napier

A city on the east coast of the North Island, known for its Art Deco architecture and wine country.

Queenstown

Queenstown is a popular South Island tourist destination known for its breathtaking scenery, adventure activities such as bungee jumping and skiing, and vibrant nightlife.

Rotorua

Rotorua's geothermal activity, which includes geysers, hot springs, and mud pools, is well-known. Maori culture, including traditional food, dance, and music, is also available to visitors.

Waiheke Island

A scenic island near Auckland, known for its vineyards, beaches, and art scene.

Waitomo Caves

The Waitomo Caves are located in the North Island and offer a unique experience to visitors with its glowworm caves and underground rivers.

Museum of New Zealand Te Papa Tongarewa

Te Papa Tongarewa is New Zealand's national museum, located in Wellington. It houses a diverse collection of exhibits and artifacts that highlight the country's natural history, cultural heritage, and art. Visitors can explore interactive exhibits, attend cultural events, and learn about New Zealand's unique history and identity.

Auckland War Memorial Museum

The Auckland War Memorial Museum, located in the heart of Auckland, is one of New Zealand's most important cultural institutions. The museum includes exhibits on New Zealand's military history, as well as displays on the country's natural history, Maori culture, and colonial history.

Waiotapu Thermal Wonderland

Waiotapu Thermal Wonderland is a geothermal park on New Zealand's North Island, near Rotorua. The park's geothermal attractions include bubbling mud pools, hot springs, and geysers. Visitors can take a self-guided walking tour of the park and see some of New Zealand's most unique and fascinating natural wonders.

Christchurch Botanic Gardens

The Christchurch Botanic Gardens are a public park in Christchurch, New Zealand's South Island. There are several themed gardens in the park, including a rose garden, a rock garden, a native New Zealand garden, and a conservatory.

Auckland

Auckland, New Zealand's largest city, is located on the North Island. It is well-known for its breathtaking natural beauty, lively culture, and diverse attractions. The city's museums, art galleries, and cultural institutions, as well as its beaches, parks, and scenic landmarks, are all open to visitors.

Coromandel Peninsula

The Coromandel Peninsula is a scenic coastal region on New Zealand's North Island. It is well-known for its beautiful beaches, clear waters, and breathtaking natural scenery. Visitors can hike the many trails in the area, go fishing, swimming, and surfing, or simply relax on the beach and soak up the sun.

Kaikoura

Kaikoura is a coastal town on New Zealand's South Island. It is well-known for its breathtaking natural beauty, particularly its diverse marine wildlife. Whale watching, swimming with dolphins, and scenic flights over the town and surrounding countryside are all options for visitors

White Island

White Island is an active volcano on New Zealand's North Island, off the coast of the Bay of Plenty. The island's crater lake, bubbling mud pools, and steam vents can all be explored on a guided tour. Witnessing the power and majesty of an active volcano is a once-in-a-lifetime opportunity.

Piha

Piha is a picturesque coastal village on the North Island, west of Auckland. It is famous for its black sand beaches, crashing surf, and breathtaking natural scenery. Hiking, swimming, and surfing are all options for visitors, or they can simply relax on the beach and take in the beauty of this rugged and unspoiled landscape.

Wanaka

Wanaka is a small town located on the South Island of New Zealand. It is known for its stunning natural beauty, particularly its crystal-clear

Tongariro National Park

Tongariro National Park is a UNESCO World Heritage site in the central North Island of New Zealand. Outdoor activities available in the park include hiking the Tongariro Alpine Crossing, skiing on Mount Ruapehu, and soaking in natural hot springs.

HIDDEN GEMS

Here are a few of these hidden gems that visitors to New Zealand should consider:

The Catlins

A rugged and remote coastal region in the southeast of the South Island with stunning waterfalls, beaches, and wildlife.

Waimangu Volcanic Valley

A geothermal wonderland near Rotorua with unique geysers, hot springs, and bubbling mud pools.

Tiritiri Matangi Island

Awildlife sanctuary off the coast of Auckland with native birds, including the rare takahe and kiwi.

Karangahake Gorge

An historic gold mining area on the North Island with scenic hiking trails, tunnels, and a suspension bridge.

Nugget Point

A scenic spot on the southeast coast of the South Island with a lighthouse, fur seals, and a stunning view of the ocean.

Lake Tekapo

A beautiful glacial lake in the Mackenzie Basin on the South Island, known for its turquoise color and stunning alpine scenery.

Cape Reinga

The northernmost point of New Zealand's North Island, where visitors can see the Tasman Sea and the Pacific Ocean collide.

Doubtful Sound

A remote and untouched fiordland in Fiordland National Park with stunning waterfalls, mountains, and wildlife.

These hidden gems offer visitors a chance to experience the natural beauty and unique culture of New Zealand off the beaten path.

MUSIC SCENE

New Zealand's music scene is diverse and vibrant, with styles and genres to suit all tastes. New Zealand has a rich musical heritage that reflects its unique culture and history, ranging from traditional Maori music to contemporary pop and rock.

Rock is a popular music genre in New Zealand, and it has produced a number of successful bands and artists over the years. These include classic acts such as Split Enz and Crowded House, as well as newer acts such as The Beths and The Phoenix Foundation. Indie, hip hop, and electronic music are also popular.

Aside from mainstream music, New Zealand has a thriving underground music scene, with a number of independent labels and venues promoting local artists. There are also a number of music festivals held throughout the year, such as Auckland's annual Laneway Festival and Gisborne's Rhythm and Vines festival.

Traditional Maori instruments such as the taonga puoro (traditional Maori musical instruments) and the kapa haka (Maori performing arts) are still practiced and celebrated in New Zealand. Many contemporary musicians incorporate Maori elements into their work, resulting in a distinct fusion of traditional and modern styles.

BEST PLACES TO SEE LIVE MUSIC

Powerstation, Auckland

This legendary music venue has hosted some of the biggest names in music over the years, including Nirvana, Radiohead, and Arctic Monkeys. Today, it continues to attract top international acts as well as up-and-coming local bands.

San Fran, Wellington

This intimate venue has a reputation for showcasing some of the best emerging talent in the country. From indie rock to electronica, San Fran has something for everyone.

Blue Smoke, Christchurch

Located in the historic Tannery complex, Blue Smoke is a charming little venue that hosts regular gigs by local and visiting artists. The atmosphere is laid-back and welcoming, and the acoustics are excellent.

The Cook, Dunedin

This quirky venue is a favorite among locals and visitors alike. The menu features tasty pub grub, and the drinks are cheap, making it the perfect place to enjoy a night out with friends.

The Cabana, Napier

With its retro decor and friendly vibe, The Cabana is a must-visit for anyone interested in New Zealand's music history. The venue has been around since the 1950s and has played host to some of the country's most legendary acts.

Isaac Theatre Royal, Christchurch

This stunningly restored theater is a favorite among music lovers for its excellent acoustics and elegant surroundings. From classical concerts to rock shows, there's always something happening at the Isaac Theatre Royal.

Meow, Wellington

This cozy little venue has a reputation for being one of the best places in town to catch up-and-coming indie acts. The menu features delicious vegetarian fare, and the beer selection is excellent.

SPORTS

Sports are an important part of New Zealand culture. The country is well-known for its love of rugby, but there are numerous other sports that have captured the nation's attention. Sports are important to New Zealanders, and the country offers a wide range of outdoor and indoor activities for both spectators and participants.

Rugby is New Zealand's national sport, and it is deeply ingrained in the country's culture. New Zealand's national rugby union team, the All Blacks, is one of the most successful sports teams in the world. Rugby union is played at every level in New Zealand, from schoolboy to professional. The Super Rugby competition, which includes teams from New Zealand, Australia, and South Africa, is one of the country's most popular sporting events.

Another popular sport in New Zealand is cricket. The Black Caps, New Zealand's national cricket team, has had great success in recent years, including reaching the final of the 2015 Cricket World Cup.

International cricket matches are also held in New Zealand at venues such as Eden Park in Auckland and the Basin Reserve in Wellington.

Soccer (football) is also popular in New Zealand. The All Whites national team has qualified for the FIFA World Cup twice. The New Zealand Football Championship, which includes teams from all over the country, is the country's own professional football league.

Netball is New Zealand's most popular female team sport. The national team, the Silver Ferns, has won the Netball World Cup four times, and the sport is popular throughout the country at all levels.

Basketball, golf, tennis, cycling, and surfing are also popular sports in New Zealand. In addition to shot putter Valerie Adams, triathlete Hamish Carter, and middle-distance runner John Walker, New Zealand has produced some world-class athletes in a variety of sports.

Aside from the sports mentioned above, New Zealand has a long history of outdoor adventure activities such as bungee jumping, skydiving, and white-water rafting. The country's stunning natural landscapes provide the ideal backdrop for these adrenaline-fueled activities, which attract tourists from all over the world.

ESSENTIAL TIPS FOR ATTENDING A GAME

Attending a sports game in New Zealand can be an exhilarating experience, especially for sports enthusiasts. Here are some tips to help you make the most of your experience:

Book your tickets in advance: Depending on the sport and team, tickets can sell out quickly. It's a good idea to book your tickets as early as possible to avoid disappointment.

Arrive early: Arrive at the stadium at least an hour before the game starts to avoid long lines and to soak up the pre-game atmosphere.

Dress appropriately: New Zealand's weather can be unpredictable, so make sure to check the weather forecast before heading out to a game. Bring warm clothing and rain gear if necessary.

Don't forget to bring cash: While many stadiums and venues do accept credit and debit cards, it's always a good idea to bring cash just in case.

Respect the culture: Sports are a big part of New Zealand culture, and it's important to respect the customs and traditions of the sport and the fans. Be polite and courteous to those around you, and don't be afraid to cheer on the home team.

Try the food: Stadium food is an important part of the game-day experience in New Zealand. Don't be afraid to try the local cuisine, such as meat pies, sausage rolls, and hot chips.

Enjoy the atmosphere: Sports games in New Zealand are known for their lively and passionate atmosphere. Take it all in, enjoy the excitement, and have fun.

Some of the best places to see live sports in New Zealand include:

Eden Park, Auckland: This is New Zealand's largest stadium and is home to the national rugby and cricket teams. It has hosted several international sporting events, including the Rugby World Cup and the Cricket World Cup.

Forsyth Barr Stadium, Dunedin: This multi-purpose stadium is home to the Otago Rugby Football Union and has hosted international rugby and football matches.

AMI Stadium, Christchurch: This stadium is home to the Crusaders rugby team and has hosted several international rugby matches.

Westpac Stadium, Wellington: This stadium is home to the Wellington Hurricanes rugby team and has hosted several international rugby and football matches.

Vector Arena, Auckland: While not a sports stadium, Vector Arena is a popular venue for concerts and other events, including basketball and boxing matches.

New Zealanders are passionate about sports, and attending a live game is a great way to experience the country's unique culture and traditions.

ITINERARY -DAY TRIPS FROM NEW ZEALAND

Waiheke Island: A 40-minute ferry ride from Auckland, Waiheke Island is famous for its vineyards, olive groves, and beautiful beaches.

Waitomo Caves: A 2.5-hour drive from Auckland, Waitomo Caves is famous for its stunning glowworm caves, underground rivers, and limestone formations.

Hobbiton: For Lord of the Rings fans, a trip to Hobbiton, the movie set where the Shire scenes were filmed, is a must. It's a 2-hour drive from Auckland.

Milford Sound: Located in the Fiordland National Park, Milford Sound is a stunning fjord that offers boat tours, kayaking, and scenic flights. It's a 4-hour drive from Queenstown.

Mount Cook: A 3-hour drive from Queenstown, Mount Cook is the highest mountain in New Zealand and offers incredible hiking trails, glacier walks, and stargazing opportunities.

Tongariro Alpine Crossing: Located in Tongariro National Park, this day hike is considered one of the best in the world. It's a 4-hour drive from Wellington.

Akaroa: A 1.5-hour drive from Christchurch, Akaroa is a picturesque French-influenced village on the Banks Peninsula that offers dolphin watching, kayaking, and swimming with dolphins.

Abel Tasman National Park: Located at the top of the South Island, Abel Tasman National Park offers stunning beaches, hiking trails, and kayaking. It's a 1.5-hour drive from Nelson.

Otago Peninsula: A 20-minute drive from Dunedin, the Otago Peninsula is home to rare wildlife such as yellow-eyed penguins, sea lions, and albatrosses.

14-DAY ITINERARY

01 DAY

Morning: Visit the Auckland War Memorial Museum and grab some local breakfast options like a traditional Māori hangi, which is a feast cooked in an underground pit oven, or some fresh fish and chips from a local fish and chip shop.

Afternoon: Head to Waiheke Island for some wine tasting and a picnic featuring local artisan cheeses and charcuterie.

Evening: Enjoy dinner at a restaurant in the Viaduct Harbour area and try some local seafood like green-lipped mussels or crayfish.

02 DAY

Morning: Take a walk around the beautiful Redwoods Treewalk and stop for a traditional Māori breakfast of porridge or fry bread with jam and honey.

Afternoon: Visit Te Puia, a Māori cultural center and see the famous Pohutu geyser before enjoying a traditional hangi lunch.

Evening: Soak in a natural hot pool at the Polynesian Spa and then head to dinner at a local pub or restaurant for some classic Kiwi pub fare like a lamb burger or fish pie.

03 DAY

Morning: Take a scenic helicopter ride over the Southern Alps and enjoy some fresh fruit and pastries for breakfast.

Afternoon: Visit a local winery for some wine tasting and enjoy a picnic with local cheese, cured meats, and fresh bread.

Evening: Head to dinner at a local restaurant and try some of New Zealand's famous lamb dishes, like a lamb rack or slow-cooked lamb shank.

04 DAY Morning: Take a boat tour of Milford Sound and enjoy a light breakfast onboard while taking in the stunning scenery.
Afternoon: Enjoy some fresh seafood for lunch at a local cafe or restaurant, such as crayfish, salmon, or blue cod.
Evening: Relax and enjoy dinner at your accommodation or grab some takeout from a local restaurant.

05 DAY Morning: Visit the Te Papa Museum and enjoy some local breakfast options like Vogel's bread with Marmite or a flat white coffee.
Afternoon: Take a stroll along the Wellington Waterfront and stop for some local craft beer and a snack at a brewery or gastropub.
Evening: Head to dinner at a local restaurant and try some traditional Kiwi comfort food like meat pies, fish and chips, or roast lamb.

06 DAY Explore the geothermal wonders of Wai-O-Tapu Thermal Wonderland
Have a traditional Māori feast at Tamaki Māori Village, featuring hangi (food cooked in an underground pit oven), poi dancing, and haka performances

07
DAY

Visit the powerful Huka Falls and take a scenic jet boat ride
Stop by L'Arte for some delicious baked goods and coffee
Enjoy a dinner of fish and chips at the iconic Dixie Brown's restaurant

08
DAY

Visit the Te Papa Tongarewa Museum to learn about New Zealand's history and culture
Take a stroll along the waterfront and stop by the local food truck park for some tasty treats
Head to Duke Carvell's for dinner, which offers a unique twist on New Zealand cuisine

09
DAY

Take a day trip to the nearby Wairarapa region, known for its wineries and artisanal food
Visit Martinborough Vineyard and enjoy a wine tasting
Have lunch at Poppies, a charming cafe featuring seasonal and locally sourced ingredients

10 DAY

Explore the charming town of Nelson and its artisanal food scene
Visit the Nelson Saturday Market for fresh produce, baked goods, and crafts
Have dinner at Hopgoods, a local favorite known for its inventive cuisine and use of local ingredients

11 DAY

Take a scenic cruise along the coastline and hike in the Abel Tasman National Park
Have lunch at The Fat Tui, a popular burger joint with a local twist
Stop by the Pic's Peanut Butter World for a sweet treat

12 DAY

Visit the Marlborough wine region and take a winery tour and tasting
Have lunch at Herzog Winery, featuring locally sourced ingredients and stunning views
Stop by the Makana Chocolate Factory for some delicious handmade chocolates

Explore the city's botanical gardens and Avon River.
Have lunch at Little High Eatery, a food hall featuring a variety of local vendors.
End the day with a dinner at Roots Restaurant, featuring an ever-changing menu based on local and seasonal ingredients.

Go whale watching and see the majestic creatures up close.
Have lunch at the Green Dolphin, a seaside restaurant featuring local seafood and produce.
Visit the Ohau Stream Walkway and see the playful seal pups.

HISTORY AND CULTURE

THE MĀORI LANGUAGE AND ITS SIGNIFICANCE IN NEW ZEALAND

Mori, also known as Te Reo Mori, is an official language of New Zealand with deep cultural significance. It is a Polynesian language spoken by New Zealand's indigenous people, the Mori, and is one of the country's three official languages, along with English and New Zealand Sign Language.

The Mori language is an essential component of Mori culture, which is deeply rooted in the Mori people's history and traditions. It is a living language that has evolved over centuries and reflects the Mori people's distinct worldview and beliefs.

The language has played an important role in preserving Mori culture and identity, and it is central to New Zealand's ongoing cultural revival of Mori traditions. Efforts are currently being made to increase the use and visibility of Te Reo Mori in everyday life, including in education, the media, and government.

Mori words and phrases are commonly used in everyday life in New Zealand, and visitors are likely to come across them in a variety of contexts. Many New Zealand place names are of Mor origin, including Auckland (Tmaki Makaurau), Wellington (Te Whanganui-a-Tara), and Christchurch (tautahi). Greetings and phrases in Te Reo Mori are also common, such as "kia ora" (hello), "whnau" (family), and "aroha" (love).

Overall, Mori plays an important role in New Zealand's national identity and cultural heritage. Visitors are encouraged to learn more about Te Reo Mori and its significance to New Zealand's people and culture.

MUSEUMS AND CULTURAL INSTITUTIONS

New Zealand has a rich cultural heritage, and this is reflected in the numerous museums and cultural institutions spread across the country. Here are some of the top museums and cultural institutions worth visiting:

Te Papa Tongarewa: This is the national museum and art gallery of New Zealand, located in Wellington. It is the largest museum in the country and houses numerous exhibitions on New Zealand's history, culture, and natural environment.

Auckland War Memorial Museum: Located in the heart of Auckland, this museum is dedicated to the history of New Zealand's involvement in wars, including the two World Wars. It also has exhibits on New Zealand's natural history and cultural heritage.

Museum of New Zealand Te Awamutu: This museum is located in the town of Te Awamutu, and it showcases the rich history and culture of the Waikato region. It has exhibits on Maori culture, early European settlement, and the region's natural history.

Otago Museum: This museum is located in Dunedin and is dedicated to the natural and cultural history of Otago and the wider southern region of New Zealand. It has exhibits on Maori culture, the natural environment, and the region's colonial history.

Canterbury Museum: Located in Christchurch, this museum has exhibits on the natural and cultural history of the Canterbury region. It includes displays on Maori culture, the region's geology and natural history, and early European settlement.

Waitangi Treaty Grounds: This is the site where the Treaty of Waitangi was signed between the Maori chiefs and the British Crown in 1840. The grounds include a museum, an interpretation center, and a marae (Maori meeting house), all of which provide insight into the significance of the treaty to New Zealand's history and culture.

Toitu Otago Settlers Museum: Located in Dunedin, this museum tells the story of the early settlers who arrived in Otago during the 19th century. It includes exhibits on Maori culture, the natural environment, and the lives of the early settlers.

These museums and cultural institutions provide a glimpse into the rich history, culture, and natural environment of New Zealand.

FAMILY-FRIENDLY ACTIVITIES

Auckland Zoo - Home to over 135 species, Auckland Zoo offers a fun and educational day out for the whole family. Get up close with the animals and learn about conservation efforts to protect them.

Te Papa Museum - New Zealand's national museum, Te Papa, offers a range of interactive exhibits for children and adults. Learn about the country's history, culture and natural environment.

Waitomo Caves - Take a guided tour of the Waitomo Caves, which are known for their incredible glowworm displays. This natural wonder is sure to leave the whole family in awe.

Zealandia Wildlife Sanctuary - Located in Wellington, Zealandia is a sanctuary for some of New Zealand's rarest wildlife. Explore the forest and see native birds, reptiles and insects in their natural habitat.

Wai-O-Tapu Thermal Wonderland - Witness the incredible geothermal activity at Wai-O-Tapu, where you can see hot springs, geysers and mud pools. This unique natural wonder is a great way to teach kids about the power of the earth.

Skyline Queenstown - Take a gondola ride up to Skyline Queenstown and enjoy panoramic views of the city and surrounding mountains. There are also family-friendly activities such as luge rides and a mountain bike park.

Puzzling World - Located in Wanaka, Puzzling World is a quirky attraction that offers a range of optical illusions and puzzles to challenge the mind. This is a great option for a rainy day.

Otago Peninsula Wildlife Tour - Take a tour of the Otago Peninsula and see native wildlife such as penguins, seals and albatross in their natural habitat. This is a great educational experience for kids.

Abel Tasman National Park - Take a hike through the beautiful Abel Tasman National Park, which offers stunning views and a chance to see native flora and fauna. There are also kayak and boat tours available to explore the coastline.

Hobbiton Movie Set Tour - Explore the world-famous movie set of Hobbiton, where the Lord of the Rings and The Hobbit trilogies were filmed. This guided tour is a must-see for any fan of the films.

TRAVELING WITH CHILDREN

TIPS FOR TRAVELING WITH KIDS

Traveling with kids can be a fun and rewarding experience, but it can also be challenging. Here are some tips to make your trip to New Zealand with kids more enjoyable:

Plan ahead: Before you leave, research family-friendly activities and accommodations. Make a list of things you want to do and see, and plan out your itinerary accordingly.

Pack smart: Pack plenty of snacks, games, and activities to keep your kids entertained during long flights or car rides. Don't forget essentials like diapers, wipes, and extra clothing.

Be flexible: Kids can be unpredictable, so be prepared to adjust your plans if needed. Allow for downtime and breaks throughout the day to avoid overtiredness and tantrums.

Choose family-friendly accommodations: When booking your accommodations, look for family-friendly hotels or vacation rentals that offer amenities such as cribs, high chairs, and play areas for children.

Involve your kids: Let your kids help plan your itinerary and choose some activities that they're interested in. This will keep them engaged and excited throughout the trip.

Stay safe: Always prioritize safety when traveling with kids. Keep an eye on them in crowded areas, hold their hand when crossing the street, and make sure they know how to contact you if they get separated.

Enjoy the journey: Remember to have fun and enjoy your time together as a family. Take lots of photos and create lasting memories that you'll treasure for years to come.

WATCHING THE SUNRISE OR SUNSET IN NEW ZEALAND

New Zealand is home to some of the most stunning natural landscapes and scenic viewpoints, making it a great destination for watching the sunrise or sunset. Here are some of the best places for watching the sunrise or sunset in New Zealand:

Cape Kidnappers, Hawke's Bay: Cape Kidnappers is a scenic headland located in Hawke's Bay that offers stunning views of the coastline. Watching the sunrise or sunset from this spot is a must-do experience.

Lake Tekapo, Canterbury: Lake Tekapo is a glacial lake located in Canterbury that is famous for its turquoise blue water and stunning scenery. Watching the sunrise or sunset from the shore of the lake is an unforgettable experience.

Milford Sound, Fiordland: Milford Sound is a fiord located in Fiordland that offers some of the most spectacular natural scenery in New Zealand. Watching the sunrise or sunset from a boat cruise in the sound is an unforgettable experience.

Mount Eden, Auckland: Mount Eden is a dormant volcano located in Auckland that offers stunning views of the city and the surrounding area. The summit is a great place to watch the sunrise or sunset.

Mount John Observatory, Canterbury: Mount John Observatory is located in the Aoraki Mackenzie Dark Sky Reserve in Canterbury and offers some of the best stargazing opportunities in the world.

Mount John Observatory, Lake Tekapo - Mount John Observatory is located on a hill overlooking Lake Tekapo and offers stunning views of the lake and surrounding mountains, particularly during sunset.

Mount Maunganui, Tauranga: Mount Maunganui is a popular holiday destination located in Tauranga that offers stunning views of the beach and the surrounding area.

Mount Victoria, Wellington - Mount Victoria provides panoramic views of Wellington and the surrounding area, making it a great spot to watch the sunrise or sunset.

Nugget Point Lighthouse, Otago: Nugget Point Lighthouse is located on the Otago coast and offers stunning views of the coastline and the surrounding area.

Roys Peak, Wanaka: Roys Peak is a popular hiking trail located near Wanaka that offers stunning views of the surrounding mountains and Lake Wanaka. Watching the sunrise or sunset from the top of the peak is an unforgettable experience.

Te Mata Peak, Hawke's Bay: Te Mata Peak is a scenic lookout located in Hawke's Bay that offers stunning views of the surrounding area.

The Remarkables, Queenstown: The Remarkables is a mountain range located near Queenstown, offering breathtaking views of the surrounding landscape.

Tunnel Beach, Dunedin - Tunnel Beach is a secluded beach surrounded by cliffs and offers a beautiful view of the coastline during sunset.

ADDITIONAL RESOURCES
LOCAL CUSTOMS AND ETIQUETTE

New Zealand has its own unique set of customs and etiquette that are important to know before visiting. Here are some examples:

- **Greetings:** Kiwis are generally friendly and approachable. When greeting someone, a firm handshake or a simple nod and smile are appropriate. The Māori culture has its own traditional greeting known as the hongi, which involves pressing noses together and inhaling.

- **Shoes:** It's common practice in New Zealand to remove your shoes before entering someone's home. Some public places, such as museums and galleries, may also require you to remove your shoes.

- **Tipping:** Tipping is not customary in New Zealand, as service charges are usually included in the bill. However, if you receive exceptional service, you may choose to leave a small tip.

- **Punctuality:** Kiwis value punctuality, so it's important to arrive on time for meetings and appointments. If you're going to be late, it's considered polite to call and let the other person know.

- **Personal space:** New Zealanders generally value their personal space, so it's important to give people their distance. This can also extend to not touching people, unless you know them well.

- **Respect for nature:** New Zealand is known for its stunning natural beauty, and Kiwis are proud of it. It's important to show respect for the environment, including not littering and being mindful of conservation efforts.

- **Māori culture:** The Māori culture is an important part of New Zealand's identity, and visitors should be aware of this. It's important to show respect for Māori customs and beliefs, including not touching a Māori person's head, as it is considered sacred.

SAFETY CONSIDERATIONS

New Zealand is generally considered a safe destination for travelers. However, it is still important to take some safety considerations into account, especially when exploring the great outdoors.

1. **Natural Hazards:** New Zealand is known for its stunning natural landscapes, but they can also pose some risks. Always check weather conditions and reports before heading out and make sure to follow any warnings or advisories from local authorities. Be aware of potential hazards such as unstable cliffs, swift rivers, and unexpected changes in weather conditions.

2. **Road Safety:** New Zealand has a good road network, but driving conditions can vary greatly depending on the location and weather conditions. Make sure to follow traffic rules and regulations, including driving on the left side of the road. Always wear a seatbelt and avoid driving under the influence of drugs or alcohol.

3. **Crime:** While New Zealand is generally safe, like any country, it is not immune to crime. Take the usual precautions such as keeping an eye on your belongings and avoiding unlit and isolated areas at night. Be aware that theft from vehicles can be common in some areas, so always lock your car and keep valuables out of sight.

4. **Water Safety:** New Zealand has a number of beautiful beaches and waterways, but they can also be dangerous. Always follow any warning signs and never swim alone or under the influence of drugs or alcohol. Be aware of rip currents and other hazards.

5. **Wildlife Safety:** New Zealand has a unique and diverse wildlife, including birds, marine mammals, and insects. While most are harmless, some can pose a risk to humans. Be aware of the risks and take appropriate precautions, such as wearing insect repellent and staying a safe distance from wildlife.

MAJOR FESTIVALS AND EVENTS IN NEW ZEALAND

Waitangi Day (February 6): Waitangi Day is a national holiday in New Zealand that commemorates the signing of the Treaty of Waitangi in 1840, which established the relationship between the Māori people and the British Crown.

Auckland Lantern Festival (February/March): The Auckland Lantern Festival is an annual event held in the weeks following the Chinese New Year. The festival features hundreds of handmade lanterns, traditional Chinese performances, and a range of food stalls.

New Zealand International Comedy Festival (April/May): The New Zealand International Comedy Festival is the largest comedy festival in the country, featuring both local and international comedians performing in venues throughout Auckland and Wellington.

Queenstown Winter Festival (June): The Queenstown Winter Festival is a 10-day celebration of winter in New Zealand, featuring a range of events including live music, street performances, and winter sports competitions.

Matariki (June/July): Matariki is a Māori festival that celebrates the rising of the Matariki star cluster, which signifies the start of the Māori New Year. The festival includes a range of cultural events, including kapa haka performances, traditional food, and storytelling.

New Zealand International Film Festival (July/August): The New Zealand International Film Festival is the largest film festival in the country, featuring a wide range of local and international films screened in cities throughout New Zealand.

All Blacks Rugby Matches (Year-round): Rugby is New Zealand's national sport, and the All Blacks are one of the country's most beloved teams. Attending an All Blacks match is a must-do for sports fans visiting New Zealand.

Toast Martinborough Wine and Food Festival (November): The Toast Martinborough Wine and Food Festival is an annual event held in the wine region of Martinborough, featuring a range of local wines, gourmet food, and live music.

NATURE RESERVES AND HIKING TRAILS

New Zealand is renowned for its natural beauty, and visitors can explore a variety of nature reserves and hiking trails throughout the country. Here are some of the most popular ones:

Fiordland National Park: Located in the southwestern part of the South Island, this park is home to Milford Sound, Doubtful Sound, and other fjords that offer stunning views of mountains, waterfalls, and wildlife.

Abel Tasman National Park: Located in the northern part of the South Island, this park is known for its golden beaches, clear waters, and hiking trails that offer views of the coastline and forested hills.

Tongariro National Park: Located in the central part of the North Island, this park is known for its volcanic landscape and hiking trails that offer views of Mount Ngauruhoe (also known as Mount Doom in the Lord of the Rings movies), Mount Tongariro, and other peaks.

Mount Cook National Park: Located in the central part of the South Island, this park is home to New Zealand's highest peak, Mount Cook (Aoraki), as well as glaciers, alpine valleys, and hiking trails that offer views of the mountains.

Te Urewera National Park:
Located in the eastern part of the North Island, this park is home to the largest area of native forest in the North Island, as well as lakes, rivers, and hiking trails that offer views of the landscape and wildlife.

Tongariro Alpine Crossing:
This is one of the most popular day hikes in New Zealand, and takes hikers through Tongariro National Park, past Mount Ngauruhoe, and across volcanic terrain with stunning views of the surrounding landscape.

Kepler Track:
Located in Fiordland National Park, this multi-day hiking trail takes hikers through a variety of landscapes, including beech forest, alpine meadows, and mountain peaks.

Routeburn Track:
This multi-day hiking trail takes hikers through Fiordland National Park and Mount Aspiring National Park, offering stunning views of mountains, lakes, and forests.

Milford Track:
This multi-day hiking trail takes hikers through Fiordland National Park, past waterfalls, lakes, and mountains, and is known as the "finest walk in the world".

Heaphy Track:
Located in Kahurangi National Park, this multi-day hiking trail takes hikers through a variety of landscapes, including forests, mountains, and coastline, and offers stunning views of the surrounding landscape.

Visitors should take care when hiking in New Zealand and ensure they are adequately prepared for the weather and terrain. It is important to follow the Department of Conservation guidelines for hiking and stay on designated trails.

SHOPPING AND MARKETS

New Zealand has a wide range of shopping options, from international brands to local boutiques and markets. Here are some of the top places to go shopping and markets to visit in New Zealand:

- **Queen Street, Auckland:** This is the main shopping street in Auckland, with a range of stores selling everything from high-end fashion to souvenirs and gifts.

- **High Street, Auckland:** Located just off Queen Street, High Street is home to a range of local boutiques and designer stores.

- **The Tannery, Christchurch:** This shopping center is housed in a historic tannery and features a range of boutiques, specialty shops, and artisan food and drink producers.

- **Cuba Street, Wellington:** This vibrant street is home to a range of vintage stores, art galleries, and independent boutiques.

- **Weta Cave, Wellington:** This is the official store of Weta Workshop, the special effects company behind movies like The Lord of the Rings and The Hobbit. Visitors can browse movie memorabilia and watch behind-the-scenes videos.

- **Christchurch Farmers' Market:** This popular weekly market features a range of local produce, artisan food products, and crafts.

- **Auckland Night Markets:** These night markets take place in various locations throughout the city and feature a range of food stalls, live music, and entertainment.

- **Matakana Farmers' Market:** This popular market is located just outside of Auckland and features a range of local produce, food, and crafts.

- **The Remarkables Market, Queenstown:** This outdoor market takes place on weekends and features a range of local produce, food, crafts, and live music.

VOLUNTEERING OPPORTUNITIES

There are many volunteering opportunities available in New Zealand, from conservation and environmental work to community development and social services. Here are some organizations that offer volunteering opportunities:

Conservation Volunteers New Zealand: This organization provides opportunities for volunteers to participate in conservation and environmental projects throughout New Zealand, including tree planting, wildlife monitoring, and habitat restoration.

New Zealand Red Cross: The New Zealand Red Cross offers volunteering opportunities in disaster response, refugee support, and community programs, such as meals on wheels and social visits for the elderly.

Habitat for Humanity New Zealand: This organization provides opportunities for volunteers to build homes and work on community development projects in partnership with families in need.

Volunteering New Zealand: This organization provides a database of volunteering opportunities throughout New Zealand, ranging from animal welfare to sports coaching to working with people with disabilities.

SPCA New Zealand: The SPCA provides opportunities for volunteers to work with animals in a variety of roles, from animal rescue and rehabilitation to education and advocacy.

Youthline New Zealand: Youthline provides opportunities for volunteers to work with young people, providing support and advice on a range of issues, including mental health and wellbeing.

Kiwi Conservation Club: This organization provides opportunities for children to participate in conservation projects and learn about New Zealand's unique flora and fauna.

DID YOU KNOW?

- New Zealand is made up of two main islands, the North Island and the South Island, as well as many smaller islands.
- New Zealand is one of the least densely populated countries in the world, with just over 5 million people living there.
- The Māori people have lived in New Zealand for over 1,000 years.
- The national symbol of New Zealand is the silver fern.
- New Zealand is home to the world's smallest dolphin, the Hector's dolphin.
- The highest mountain in New Zealand is Mount Cook, which is over 3,700 metres tall.
- The longest place name in New Zealand is Taumatawhakatangihangakoauauotamateaturipukakapikimaungah oronukupokaiwhenuakitanatahu.
- New Zealand has three official languages: English, Māori, and New Zealand Sign Language.
- New Zealand was the first country in the world to give women the right to vote.
- New Zealand has no snakes, venomous insects, or dangerous wild animals.
- The kiwi bird is native to New Zealand and is flightless.
- The official currency of New Zealand is the New Zealand dollar.
- The longest river in New Zealand is the Waikato River.
- The Beehive in Wellington is the executive wing of the New Zealand Parliament.
- New Zealand is the only country to have two national anthems.
- New Zealand is home to the world's largest flightless parrot, the kakapo.
- New Zealand has more Scottish pipe bands per capita than any other country in the world.
- The Treaty of Waitangi was signed in 1840 and is considered New Zealand's founding document.

- The New Zealand All Blacks rugby team has one of the best winning records in the world.
- New Zealand is home to the world's only alpine parrot, the kea.
- New Zealand has a reputation for being one of the most environmentally friendly countries in the world.
- The New Zealand Department of Conservation manages over 8 million hectares of land.
- The New Zealand fur seal is one of the rarest seals in the world.
- The New Zealand dollar is often called the "kiwi" because of the bird that appears on the one-dollar coin.
- The New Zealand green gecko is one of the most distinctive geckos in the world.
- New Zealand was one of the last places on Earth to be settled by humans.
- New Zealand is home to the world's only flightless parrot, the kakapo.
- New Zealand has a reputation for being one of the friendliest countries in the world.
- The North Island of New Zealand is home to the world's largest hot spring, the Frying Pan Lake.
- The New Zealand falcon is the country's only native falcon.
- New Zealand has one of the highest rates of home ownership in the world.
- The New Zealand silver fern is a symbol of the country and is used on the national rugby team's jerseys.
- The New Zealand kea is the world's only alpine parrot.
- New Zealand is home to the world's smallest penguin, the little penguin.
- The New Zealand fantail is one of the most common birds in the country.
- The Kauri tree is native to New Zealand and can grow up to 50 metres tall.
- The New Zealand tuatara is one of the world's oldest living reptiles.
- New Zealand is home to many unique species

CONCLUSION

Finally, New Zealand is a destination that offers something for everyone. Tourists will have a memorable experience in New Zealand, with its stunning natural landscapes and outdoor activities, as well as its rich Maori culture, delectable cuisine, and friendly people. There are numerous options to explore and enjoy whether you are traveling alone, with friends, or with family.

Visitors to New Zealand can expect to be greeted by friendly locals who are eager to provide advice and assistance. The well-developed infrastructure of the country makes it simple to navigate and travel between destinations. Its diverse range of accommodation options, from luxurious hotels and resorts to cozy bed and breakfasts and backpacker hostels, caters to every budget and preference.

The country's unique flora and fauna, including the famous kiwi bird, make it a must-see for nature enthusiasts. Its numerous national parks and hiking trails offer a never-ending supply of adventure and exploration. Furthermore, its vibrant arts and music scenes, as well as its numerous cultural events and festivals, provide an opportunity to immerse oneself in the country's rich cultural heritage.

A trip to New Zealand promises to be a once-in-a-lifetime experience that will leave you with lasting memories. So pack your bags, prepare for adventure and discovery, and prepare to be enchanted by the beauty and wonder of this incredible destination.

GUIDE IN SUMMARY - FAQ

- **Do I need a visa to visit New Zealand?**
  - It depends on your nationality and the purpose of your visit. Check the New Zealand Immigration website or contact the nearest New Zealand embassy or consulate to determine if you need a visa.
- **What is the best time to visit New Zealand?**
  - The best time to visit New Zealand depends on your interests. Summer (December to February) is ideal for outdoor activities, while winter (June to August) is great for skiing and snowboarding.
- **What is the currency in New Zealand?**
  - The currency in New Zealand is the New Zealand Dollar (NZD).
- **Is New Zealand a safe country to travel to?**
  - Yes, New Zealand is considered one of the safest countries in the world for travelers. However, it's essential to exercise the usual precautions, like being aware of your surroundings and belongings.
- **What should I pack for my trip to New Zealand?**
  - Your packing list should depend on the season and activities you plan to do. Be prepared for changing weather, and include clothing for both warm and cold conditions.
- **Is it necessary to get travel insurance for New Zealand?**
  - Travel insurance is highly recommended when visiting New Zealand. It can help cover medical emergencies, trip cancellations, and other unexpected events.
- **What are the must-visit destinations in New Zealand?**
  - Popular destinations include Auckland, Wellington, Queenstown, Christchurch, Rotorua, and the beautiful landscapes of the South Island, including Milford Sound and Fiordland National Park.

FAQ...

- **How can I get around New Zealand?**
  - New Zealand has an extensive network of roads, and you can rent a car or use buses for transportation. Domestic flights and ferries are also available for longer distances between the North and South Islands.
- **Do I need any vaccinations to enter New Zealand?**
  - New Zealand typically does not require vaccinations for entry, but it's advisable to check with your local healthcare provider and the New Zealand Ministry of Health for any updated health requirements.
- **What are the customs regulations when entering New Zealand?**
  - New Zealand has strict biosecurity regulations. Declare any food, plant, or animal products when you arrive, and be aware of the rules to prevent the introduction of pests and diseases.
- **Can I use my mobile phone in New Zealand?**
  - Most international mobile phones work in New Zealand, but it's essential to check your roaming plan with your provider or consider getting a local SIM card for more cost-effective options.
- **What is the voltage and plug type in New Zealand?**
  - New Zealand uses 230-240V electricity with Type I plug sockets. If your devices use a different plug type or voltage, you may need a power adapter or converter.
- **What are some popular outdoor activities in New Zealand?**
  - New Zealand offers various outdoor activities, including hiking (tramping), skiing, snowboarding, kayaking, bungee jumping, and exploring its stunning national parks.
- **What are some traditional New Zealand foods to try?**
  - Be sure to sample iconic New Zealand dishes like Pavlova (a dessert), Hangi (a traditional Maori feast), and seafood such as green-lipped mussels and fish and chips.

BUCKET LIST

- **Explore the Fiordland:** Cruise through Milford Sound or Doubtful Sound, surrounded by breathtaking fiords, waterfalls, and lush rainforests.
- **Hike the Tongariro Alpine Crossing:** Trek across this iconic trail in Tongariro National Park, passing volcanic craters, emerald lakes, and dramatic scenery.
- **Visit Hobbiton:** Take a guided tour of the Hobbiton Movie Set, a must for any "Lord of the Rings" and "Hobbit" film series fan.
- **Admire the Glowworm Caves:** Explore the magical Waitomo Caves and witness thousands of glowworms illuminating the underground.
- **Experience Maori Culture:** Attend a traditional Maori cultural performance, including a Hangi feast, to learn about New Zealand's indigenous culture.
- **Go Whale Watching:** Head to Kaikoura for a chance to see sperm whales, orcas, and other marine life on a whale-watching tour.
- **Skydiving in Queenstown:** Take a leap of faith and skydive over the stunning landscapes of Queenstown, known as the "Adventure Capital of the World."
- **Hot Air Balloon Ride:** Soar over the picturesque landscapes of Canterbury or Waikato in a hot air balloon for a unique perspective.
- **Relax in Natural Hot Springs:** Soak in the geothermal hot springs of Rotorua or Hanmer Springs, known for their healing properties.
- **Bungee Jumping at Kawarau Bridge:** Try the original bungee jump at Kawarau Bridge, where it all began.
- **Tramp the Routeburn Track:** A multi-day hike through Fiordland and Mount Aspiring National Parks, offering stunning alpine scenery.
  - Visit Aoraki / Mount Cook: Explore New Zealand's highest peak and the surrounding Southern Alps with hiking, stargazing, and glacier tours.

BUCKET LIST

- **Swim with Dolphins:** Encounter playful dolphins in the Bay of Islands or Akaroa, and even have the opportunity to swim with them.
- **See the Southern Lights:** If you're lucky, witness the Southern Lights (Aurora Australis) in the night sky, particularly in the southernmost regions.
- **Wine Tasting in Marlborough:** Sample some of New Zealand's finest wines in the Marlborough region, famous for its Sauvignon Blanc.
- **Cruise the Abel Tasman Coast:** Explore the Abel Tasman National Park by kayak or boat, discovering secluded beaches and crystal-clear waters.
- **Visit the Franz Josef and Fox Glaciers:** Take a guided glacier hike or scenic flight over these stunning ice formations.
- **Mountain Biking in Rotorua:** Experience thrilling mountain biking trails in the Rotorua Redwoods Forest.
- **Explore the Otago Peninsula:** Spot rare wildlife like albatross, penguins, and seals in this beautiful coastal area.
- **Attend a Rugby Match:** Immerse yourself in New Zealand's rugby culture by attending a local rugby match, especially if the All Blacks are playing.
- **Sail the Bay of Islands:** Charter a sailboat and explore the stunning bays, islands, and marine life of the Bay of Islands.
- **Take a Scenic Train Ride:** Enjoy a scenic train journey on the TranzAlpine or Taieri Gorge Railway, offering stunning vistas.
- **Stroll through Wellington's Te Papa Museum:** Discover New Zealand's history, art, and culture at the interactive Te Papa Tongarewa Museum.

BACKPACKING IN NEW ZEALAND

Where to Stay:

1. **Hostels:** Hostels are the go-to accommodation for budget travelers. They offer dormitory-style rooms and often have communal kitchens, lounges, and social activities. Some popular hostel chains in New Zealand include YHA, Nomads, and Base Backpackers.

2. **Camping:** New Zealand has many scenic campsites, some of which are free or low-cost. Be sure to check regulations and respect the environment while camping. Department of Conservation (DOC) campsites are a good option.

3. **Budget Motels and Holiday Parks:** If you want a bit more comfort without breaking the bank, consider staying in budget motels or holiday parks. They often provide self-catering facilities and communal areas.

4. **Couchsurfing:** Connect with locals through Couchsurfing to find free accommodation and gain insights into New Zealand's culture.

BACKPACKING IN NEW ZEALAND:

Surviving on a Budget:

1. **Cook Your Own Meals:** Save money by preparing your meals. Hostel kitchens and campgrounds typically have cooking facilities. Take advantage of local markets for fresh produce.

2. **Use Public Transportation:** New Zealand has an extensive bus network, and hop-on-hop-off bus passes are popular among backpackers. Consider a backpacker bus pass for flexibility and affordability.

3. **Carpooling and Hitchhiking:** If you're comfortable with it, hitchhiking is a common practice in New Zealand and can be a cost-effective way to get around. Alternatively, check ridesharing platforms for carpooling options.

4. **Multi-Attraction Passes:** Look for multi-attraction passes, such as the New Zealand Explorer Pass, which offers discounts on various attractions.

5. **Free and Low-Cost Activities:** Take advantage of New Zealand's natural beauty. Many of the best activities, like hiking, beachcombing, and exploring national parks, are either free or very affordable.

BACKPACKING IN NEW ZEALAND

Making Money While Traveling:

1. **Working Holiday Visa:** If you're aged 18-30 (or 35 for some countries), consider applying for a working holiday visa. It allows you to work and travel in New Zealand for a specified period.

2. **Temporary Jobs:** Look for temporary jobs in industries like hospitality, agriculture, and tourism. Many backpackers find work in fruit picking, bar staff, or as ski instructors during the winter season.

3. **WWOOFing:** Join the Worldwide Opportunities on Organic Farms (WWOOF) program, where you can exchange work on farms for accommodation and meals.

4. **Seasonal Work:** Depending on the season, opportunities exist for seasonal work such as grape picking, kiwifruit harvesting, and cherry picking.

5. **Freelancing and Remote Work:** If you have skills that can be done online, consider freelancing or remote work to sustain your travels.

6. **Volunteer Opportunities:** Many organizations and conservation projects in New Zealand accept volunteers in exchange for room and board. Check out websites like Workaway and HelpX.

My Safety Plan

1 My warning signs are:

2 My effective coping strategies are:

3 People I can reach out to for distraction:

4 People I can reach out to for help:

Remember: Help is always available.

5 Steps I can take to make my environment safer. Please list:

6 In the event of a crisis:
Call Emergency Contact #1:
Call Crisis Hotline:
Call Emergency Services:

Travel Packing List

Documents	Clothes	Personal Care

Tech	Travel	Others

Travel Packing List

Documents

Clothes

Personal Care

Tech

Travel

Others

Travel Packing List

Documents	Clothes	Personal Care

Tech	Travel	Others

TRAVEL

DATE:

DURATION:

DESTINATION:

PLACES TO SEE:

1 _____
2 _____
3 _____
4 _____
5 _____
6 _____
7 _____

LOCAL FOOD TO TRY:

1 _____
2 _____
3 _____
4 _____
5 _____
6 _____
7 _____

DAY 1	DAY 2	DAY 3

DAY 4	DAY 5	DAY 6

NOTES

EXPENSES IN TOTAL:

PLANNER

TRAVEL

DATE:

DURATION:

DESTINATION:

PLACES TO SEE:	LOCAL FOOD TO TRY:
1 _____	1 _____
2 _____	2 _____
3 _____	3 _____
4 _____	4 _____
5 _____	5 _____
6 _____	6 _____
7 _____	7 _____

DAY 1	DAY 2	DAY 3

DAY 4	DAY 5	DAY 6

NOTES	EXPENSES IN TOTAL:

PLANNER

TRAVEL

DATE:

DURATION:

DESTINATION:

PLACES TO SEE:	LOCAL FOOD TO TRY:
1 _____	1 _____
2 _____	2 _____
3 _____	3 _____
4 _____	4 _____
5 _____	5 _____
6 _____	6 _____
7 _____	7 _____

DAY 1	DAY 2	DAY 3

DAY 4	DAY 5	DAY 6

NOTES	EXPENSES IN TOTAL:

PLANNER

NOTES

S M T W T F S

NOTES

NOTES

S M T W T F S

NOTES

DATE   S M T W T F S

NOTES

S M T W T F S

NOTES

NOTES

S M T W T F S

NOTES

S M T W T F S

NOTES

NOTES

S M T W T F S

NOTES

S M T W T F S

IMAGE CREDITS

Please be aware that, while we have made every effort to properly credit all photographs used in this travel guide, we sincerely apologize for any inadvertent omissions. If you believe your photo has been used without your permission, please contact us at harrisonwalshawtravels@gmail.com right away and we will make the necessary changes.

Printed in Great Britain
by Amazon

31395912R00056